TWO REGULAR GUYS

by

One of Them

ELAINE CHAYTOR

Edited by Claire Garnett

June Fraser and Elaine Chaytor 'Two Regular Guys'.

First Published 2005.
© Copyright Claire Garnett 2005.
Published by Manor Publications.

ISBN 0-9537206-1-6 (978-0-9537206-1-3)

Printed by Kelso Graphics
The Knowes, Kelso, Scottish Borders TD5 7BH. Tel: 01573 223214

CONTENTS

FOREWORD

Elaine Chaytor was born in 1904. Her father, the Rev. Henry John Chaytor, was a gifted academic, whose career led through the ministry and teaching to his many years as Fellow and Master of St Catherine's College, Cambridge. Her mother, Mary Pinwill, was the third daughter of the Rev. Edmund Pinwill of Ermington and, like her six sisters, she was an artistic and enthusiastic little lady. Mary was one of the Rashleigh Pinwill woodcarvers, set up and run by the sisters, producing beautiful and original woodcarvings for churches all over the West Country, which can still be enjoyed today.

Elaine's first book, *Ermington Days*, tells of her childhood in rural Devonshire a century ago. Written for today's children, life in and around the vicarage comes vividly to life putting the reader intimately in touch with a vanished age. The book also introduces her extended family, many of whom were artists, musicians and craftsmen.

When Elaine graduated from Cambridge University with a good degree in French, her family looked to see her embrace an academic career. But in her body and soul she lived for dancing and in this they wholeheartedly supported her. Only then did she take the opportunity to train as a dancer, her late start carried through by her natural gift and enthusiasm. But the regime of the corps de ballet was not for her. Elaine and her friend, *June*, devised their own 'sister act' and trod the variety circuit all over Britain, Ireland and on the Continent.

Two Regular Guys is a lively description of the two girls' adventures travelling the country from theatre to theatre, dancing in cabarets and clubs and coping with unusual situations in Europe. The 1930s saw the last years of traditional variety. Artists struggled through the depression and the popularity of the new cinemas threatened the viability of live performance.

Elaine describes the old theatres, many now long gone; digs and dressing rooms; customers and landladies; agents and artists; and memorable characters on stage and in the wings. The two girls were warm hearted, with a great sense of humour. Wherever they danced they had tremendous fun, made good friends and always saw the best in the most unpromising situation. Perhaps this was the key to their success and enjoyment of their dancing career.

Elaine and June's dancing career round the variety circuit took place from 1933 to 1936. In April 1937 Elaine went with her parents on an Hellenic cruise to Greece, where she met her future husband, Charles Trinder. They were married in June of that year and settled in Banstead, Surrey, where two daughters, Claire and Marcia, were born. Bringing up children in the war years effectively put a stop to Elaine's dancing. After the war, the family moved to rural Hertfordshire and Elaine was able to keep in touch with the world of ballet in London as well as being involved in local amateur dramatics, where her talent for choreography, costume making and script writing were put to good use. Daily ballet exercises throughout her life kept her dancing muscles in good trim, their place being taken in her later years by a regular yoga routine.

In 1994, five years after the death of her husband, she moved to Scotland to be near her elder daughter in Manor Valley, Peebles. It was here, at the age of 92, that she wrote *Two Regular Guys*, her memories as fresh as ever. Elaine Chaytor died on her 93rd birthday, July 19th 1997.

Claire Garnett
Daughter of Elaine Chaytor

Elaine Chaytor.

CHAPTER I

OVERTURE

It is 1930 and the Jeunesse Dore of the land are still captivated by the Ballet Russe. Diagliev has been ferried to the funeral island in the Venice lagoon and his company disbanded, but with new productions and in various guises Russian ballet goes on. We love it! We queue for hours in Floral Street, St Martin's Lane. We collect programmes. We know all the ballerinas by name and have our favourites. We dance ourselves whenever possible, in amateur operas and even in ballrooms.

One day there arrives in the university town of Cambridge, a young don with a beautiful wife who, not so long ago, was a top dancer in the Russian school, working in the companies of Pavlova and Korsavina. Naturally all the balletomanes are delighted when, missing her terpsichorean past, Georgie starts a ballet club.

Here we are now, a very curious assortment of young people, working away at ballet. By and by we put together a little show. Georgie is very clever at arranging simple but effective numbers for us and does several solos herself so it is a great success.

Georgie has a ballet friend visiting her who naturally comes to see our show. She comes to me and says,

"You are a natural dancer. You should really have some lessons. I can fix you up to go to my old teacher, Princess Astafieva. She has a dance studio in Chelsea."

I have absolutely no thought of a stage career. I consider that my shape is all wrong, but I love dancing above all else and this sounds wonderfully exciting.

Astafieva had been a member of the pre-war Russian Ballet and was an inspired, if eccentric teacher. Markova and Polin were certainly trained by her. Every dancer of note from Ninette de Valois to Penelope Spencer came back from time to time. When Pavlova wanted recruits for her company, it was to Madame she always went.

So here I am at the Pheasantry, a beautiful Georgian house in the Kings Road. The studio is on the first floor, a big, sunny room with long windows giving onto little balconies with fancy iron railings. The long wall facing the barre is all mirror. Many dancers, rainbow like in their bright practice costumes, are trying out steps, or standing chatting. After a long wait madam appears.

Madam is dressed in a black petticoat hitched up with elastic, a dilapidated shawl turban-wise on her head, her legs encased in whitish, woolly leggings. She holds a long, black stick in one hand and a cigarette in the other. She smokes non-stop.

Lessons are conducted in a mixture of execrable English and rapid Russian. They start when she feels like it and stop when she has had enough. The class is not as full as I had expected. The lack of anything like a timetable makes it difficult for dancers who are working and *do* have an exact timetable. The make up of the class is a bit strange, too. In most schools pupils are graded by ability but here anyone can join in who has an introduction and 7/6, the cost of a lesson.

It is not easy to follow Madam's instructions; she often explains a step by dancing her fingers on the piano lid. Sometimes she flies into a terrible rage, banging ankles with her stick and reducing some poor sinner to floods of tears. She could also be very kind to anyone who really tried.
"Elaine never forget a step," she says to me.
Class is rather like a salon. Old friends drop in for a chat and to watch the stars in the front line performing with terrific brio. They ignore the bumblers at the back.
I can only afford one lesson a week but the hours I spend there are the happiest in my life. Though I cannot afford much teaching, I keep practicing at home and am improving a lot.

It is now Autumn and one of the other back row dancers says to me,
"I am going to audition for panto this afternoon. Why don't you come along and have a go?"
This sounded interesting so I go along with her to a big, gloomy room full of girls in practice dress. We change and give our names. Presently my name is called and I go forward. A depressed looking man sits at the piano.
"Got your music?" he asks.
Oh dear! No music! I ask him to play a waltz and manage to put a few steps together. A rather harassed looking man says,
"Wait over there."
Soon I find myself standing in line with eleven other girls. I have got a job! This is quite unexpected but I have nothing on at this time, so why not give it a go?

The panto is *Babes in the Wood*, twice nightly in Croydon, but rehearsals are in Soho. The ballets, and other numbers, are arranged by a very lively old bird called Judith Espinosa. She shouts at us a good deal, but she knows what she is about. Things are turning out well.

At last it is the dress rehearsal in the theatre, which goes on and on. We sit in the stalls yawning but as last the show is ready.

Babes in the Wood can be cast in several ways. Sometimes the 'babes' are played by two comics, but in this show the two comics, a well known variety duo, play the robbers and the "babes" are children. The boy babe, actually a girl, looks about eight or nine years old, the girl babe a bit younger. But wait a minute! She is over there having a big argument with her agent. This is no child but a well-known midget act – "Baby Love". She earns her scratch by being carried through the auditorium in a fancy box, which is handed by the conductor to a stooge onstage, who is naturally astounded when the doll he unpacks from the box goes into a song and dance routine. Baby Love is about twenty five and the other children find her very strange. There are a lot of children in the show. As well as the actors and the understudies there are Miss Somebody-or-Other's Twenty Tiny Tots. Tot control is good, the trouble being that there are so many. There are also singers, comics, showgirls, acrobats and dancers. The dressing rooms are packed. You can hardly make up and there is no-where to sit down. We go back stage and perch on bits of scenery. In our lovely sylphide dresses we look like a Degas painting.

We do not have much time for sitting about. As well as dancers, we are jolly villagers, naughty schoolgirls, castle retainers and anything else they can think up. In spite of the pressure there is a very cheery atmosphere backstage. The comics are great at playing jokes and making everyone laugh. One night the Baron is doing a mock fight and ends up with a flourish, sticking his sword through one of the flats. The other side, on stage, is a showgirl posing as a statue. Did that statue come to life!

The pantomime is over now, so what to do next?

"I know a Miss Bradshaw, who gets up troops," says a very nice girl called Morwenna, "Would any of you like to come along and see if she has anything?"

Some of us go along to see what goes.

"I have some work in view," says the lady, "But I can't afford to pay you for rehearsals."

Some of the girls go off but Morwenna and I decide to give it a try. Miss B. gets some other girls and makes up a troupe of eight. We do four kicking numbers, very boring but good exercise. Presently she has some dates and hires costumes.

The dates Miss B. fixes are all over the place, in London and in the outer suburbs, at clubs, parties, restaurants, galas; they are one-night stands only, but we make enough to live on. There are also auditions for concert parties to attend. All the girls want to get into one of these – three month's work in a lovely(?) seaside town like Margate or Blackpool. Luckily I am not so keen on this as I do not get chosen at any of the auditions so I decide to go home for the summer. I would like to take some ballet lessons but Madame is unwell and the studio closed.

It is Autumn again and I apply for a job with the *Babes in the Wood* management. I am engaged as one of the dancers in Mother Goose, out of town at Eastbourne, Brighton and Hastings. We rehearse in London. The ballets are not much fun and the choreographer seems to know very little about the art. That does not worry the producer and it turns out to be a very bright and jolly show. The comics never stop trying to be funny; the second girl (boy) is very nice but takes her solo song very seriously. The comics are determined to make her laugh. One night they all dress up as yokels in wigs and beards and sit in the front stalls making corny remarks.
"Cor! Look at 'er! She be good."
"Nah! She aint no good. Not bad legs tho'."
"That's not like no boy I iver see, thank Gawd. Gid orf! Gid orf!"
She never dried up, not even on the last night when they sent a green clockwork crocodile across the stage and it sat quacking at her feet.
The dressing rooms are of course packed out, so a friend and I flee backstage, climb into the flies to chat with a lovely old man in a bowler hat with a walrus moustache and a strong Sussex accent.
"My dearrrs," he says, "I'll tell ye a story what 'appened round yerr years and years past."
He gets so deep into his story that he misses his cue and forgets to drop a piece of scenery on time. The stage manager is furious but it doesn't worry the old boy.
"Ar, er stuck er did. They pull er oop too high an I cudna git her down no'ow. I shuck an I shuck an er come down all sideways like."
On the last night he brings us some of his own rhubarb wine. Gosh! What a kick! We can hardly dance our numbers.

Eastbourne is very pleasant. The family come and stay in a hotel for Christmas. The weather is mild so we can enjoy walks on the downs and paddling in the sea.
Brighton is a bit dull but we like Hastings — a very interesting old town with fishermen to watch and fascinating caves. The show is enlivened by the eccentric behaviour of the scenery, which hadn't travelled well. Flats suddenly fall down, doors, which should have opened don't and the grand staircase has got so rickety that on the finale every single character coming down to take their bow, trips and nearly falls. This is a hilarious end to the show.

CHAPTER II

FIRST ACT

A group of us are discussing what to do next. Concert party jobs are hard to get, especially now that many managements are hiring a block of Tiller girls, numbers, costumes and all instead of individuals who have to be taught and dressed. I begin to think about putting together and act. Another girl has the same idea. She is only seventeen and very provincial. She comes from Manchester and has a great regional accent. Her name is June Fraser. (Actually her name is Annie Nuttall, but she doesn't like it.)

June and I get back to town and take digs together in Brixton. This is a great place to live if you haven't much money. The houses are big and old, with large rooms and gardens. We have a ground floor with access to same. The whole atmosphere is very relaxed – quite the Latin Quarter. No one notices if you go shopping in pyjamas. There is a late night tram from the Embankment, so you always get home, however late your show. At the end of Crowhurst Road, where we live, there is an all-night coffee stall in a converted caravan. At almost any time you can get a hot Tikky-Snack pie, a bun and a cup of coffee for 9d, and feel well fed. We eat there so often we become friends of the owner and are invited to eat our pies in the inner sanctum where his friends forgather. They are a very dodgy lot though polite and friendly. If the night patrolling policeman stops for a warming drink he is not invited in. When the lock of our trunk jams, it is opened in a trice by Two Gun Steve, who we understand to be a burglar.

There are some pretty odd characters in the digs, too. One is a retired naval officer with shell shock. He shakes all the time and at night prowls about trying to get into people's rooms. Another is a very gentlemanly ex-jail bird, who has done time for assaulting small boys. He is always looking over his shoulder.

To put together an act you need some ideas, some music and some costumes. You also need to eat, so we go along to see Miss Bradshaw and join the troupe she is getting up. It is the same boring set-up as before but now June and I do solo turns, which is more fun.

We have now worked out a programme, decided on our music and begun to rehearse in our room and in the garden. We can't afford a room or a pianist so we sing the music. We are no great shakes as singers. June says, "We must do ballet and tap."

"I am not much good at tap," I answer. "I have hardly done any."

"I will teach you," she says.

The Hornpipe Novelty dance.

June is a good teacher and seems to have studied every kind of dance at her school.

Presently we go up to Brixton market to buy fabrics and borrow the landlord's ancient sewing machine to make our costumes.

For the ballet we have royal blue feathered bras and pants and frilly organdie skirts; for the tap green satin pants with wide sleeved tops. For the last number, a comic hornpipe, we get red, white and blue oilcloth and American sailor hats. June is very good at dressmaking.

We go to Soho, where there are many music publishers, for our band parts. The Blue Danube and the Hornpipe we have to buy but we are given free copies of a number of pop tunes, one of which we shall use for the tap. The cutting out of the relevant bits of music is left to me.

Now we must get an audition, so off to that celebrated rendezvous of the variety profession, Lyons Tea Shop in Charing Cross Road. We get chatting to a few friends who have various suggestions.

"Cabaret is what you want. Percy does cabaret. Go and see him. He'll fix you up."

"No. Stanley Goldman has much more work. Better class too. . . ."

We go to see Percy Lee.

"You can do your act at the Paradise Club. No money, mind, but I will come and see it. If it is any good, I'll probably be able to fix you something."

We do not mind about the money. It is so much better to be seen in a proper setting, not in a gloomy rehearsal room with a depressed pianist thumping at your music all wrong on a tinny piano.

The Paradise Club is small but cheerful. We are on very late, without a run through but the small band is quite confident. We get through our show reasonably well in spite of a slightly jazzy Blue Danube. Percy Lee is there.

"Quite nice, girls. I'd like to see you again at the Queen's Club. Can you do next Thursday?"

"We'll be there, thank you Mr Lee."

The act goes quite well at this club too. As we are changing a lady comes into the dressing room.

"I like your act, kids. You should do well. I know how hard it is starting. Take this to help with your costumes." She then thrusts £3 into my hands. She was in the business herself, sister of a famous musical comedy star.

Percy Lee books us for a week at a restaurant.

"The money's not much, only £4, but it's a start. I will waive my commission."

This date leads to others in a variety of venues; West End clubs; very late one-night stands out in the sticks; sometimes another restaurant. We like these; they are so odd. Sometimes we have to change in a pantry or passage quite near the kitchens. The waiters, though rushed, are kindly and give us a lot of goodies. I have often run on swallowing the last bit of a cream cake. The money is not much and it is tiring lugging our cases to all these venues and getting home so late.

One night we are trudging down to the Embankment for the last tram, when a taxi pulls up beside us.

"Don't be funny! We can't afford taxis."

"I know you dancing girls. I'm knocking off now – going to the Brixton garage. Hop in for a free ride!" A very kind man.

One day a surprise.

"I've booked you girls for two weeks variety; one week at Barstow, one at Wakefield, £8 each week. Sign the contract here, and as it is such short notice you'll get your confirmation from the managers."

This is great! Just what we have been hoping for.

"We are now real variety pros. Let's hope we don't mess things up."

The following Monday we take an early train to Barstow.

For several years, before all this theatrical business started, I had owned a little dog, a Sealyham called George, who went absolutely everywhere with me. He was a very sociable, easy-going chap who liked and was liked by everybody. So when he became a theatrical dog he fitted in very well. He guarded our dressing room while we were on stage. Sometimes we could hear him barking in the distance as we worked and we knew that he was repelling boarders. There was never any need to lock our dressing room while George guarded our possessions. He was also very clever in towns. If, at the beginning of the week, we walked from our digs to the theatre and on coming out had forgotten the way back, George knew the way back, crossing every street at the exact place we had crossed when coming the other way. I am sure he thought we were very silly.

If we were working in some town where it would be quite difficult to take him for proper walks or in London doing a lot of cabaret and of course when we were abroad, he was quite happy to stay with my mother in Cambridge. They got on extremely well together.

Sometime after I left the stage, George died of heart trouble, aged ten.

CHAPTER III

IT WON'T SHOW FROM THE FRONT!

There are quite few things it is as well to know about a variety engagement. Let us see how a seasoned pro would comport himself.

He will have booked his digs in advance, having got an address either from a friend or from the stage doorkeeper, who keeps a list of addresses given him by hopeful landladies.

He will arrive on Sunday evening. Having given the stage doorkeeper his E.T.A., he will be met at the station by the theatre baggage man who will whisk away his baskets and cases and convey them to the theatre where they will be locked in the dressing room our pro will occupy during the week. He can now have a restful evening having a meal in his digs, looking up old friends who might be working locally and checking out the likely pubs.

Next morning he is at the theatre quite early, gets his key, unlocks his dressing room and his basket and rootles about for his band books. Then it is up onto the gloomy, empty stage. He plonks his music right at the front on the prompt side. Good! He is the first.

As the other acts arrive they in turn put down their music beside his until there is a long line. Soon the conductor, the pianist and a few instrumentalists turn up but not a complete orchestra. Many of the players are busy during the day in their shops or offices. Pit orchestras in provincial towns are only semi-professional. They consist mostly of elderly, amateur but keen instrumentalists: the grocer, the chemist, the undertaker etc and the occasional young man who likes to blow a trumpet, trombone or other noisy instrument. These groups are not always very expert but they simply love playing and woe to the artist who does not have all the correct band parts.

Woe also to artists who are late arrivals, and are bottom of the list. The conductor is looking at his watch, some of the players are putting by their instruments. It is time for lunch. It is a sad thing that the coming of Equity made theatre bands expensive, and they have vanished forever.

Our pro, having had his run through, goes in search of the Stage Manager. Ordinary acts do not have any scenery but rely on what the theatre can provide and the Stage Manager has to sort out how much stage each requires and what kind of backdrop they would like. Some need full stage, some half and some will work in a front cloth. Singers do not like noisy props being set up behind them. Dancers do not like conjurers who leave bits of paper, rice and damp patches behind them.

The Stage Manager has a number of backdrops on offer; many a bit the worse for wear. Who would like a garden drop? The street? The palace? Or the plain tabs? Our pro, who is the first, gets the best deal and now he is off to see the electrician with his lighting plot. Where is the electrician? Probably in the flies or up front in the projection box – presently he is found and consulted. Our pro, his lighting approved, goes off to his dressing room to unpack.

First he hangs up a dustsheet to protect his costumes from the grimy walls; another one to cover them and similar treatment for the dressing table. All is ready and he can go off to lunch and an afternoon nap.

Fraser & Chaytor, as we now call ourselves, do things a bit differently. Having taken an early train we arrive about mid-morning. We lug our heavy cases to the theatre, find the stage door and the doorkeeper, who gives us a key. "Dressing Room Six – along there, girls."

Dressing Room six is a small, ill lit cubicle. We unpack our band book and go on stage. A busy looking man with a clip board comes up.

"You must be *'Fraser and Chaytor'.* Thought ye wer'nt coming. Other acts is all here. You're on first. Half stage. What sort of drop d'you want?"

"Could we have some plain tabs?"

"Nah. Conjurer's get them. Can do you a nice country drop, or the rustic interior – or the palace?"

"We'll settle for the country drop, thankyou. Do we really have to be first?"

"Always start with a dumb act while people are coming in. 'Ave you seen the electrician?"

We go and see the electrician. He is annoyed we have no plot but in spite of this he does some very inspired lighting when we are on stage.

Well, now our band call comes up. We are last, it is late and the conductor is far from genial. He says our music is a muddle and doesn't know how he'll get through it. Not surprising really. No-one seems to want us any more so we unpack and set off to see about some digs armed with a list of addresses produced by the all-providing doorman.

Now, this is the great Thirties Depression. Many people are out of work so some take to letting rooms – sacrificing their treasured front rooms for a little mazuma. The first address we try is full up. The second can take us. It is a rather run down looking terrace house of Victorian aspect but it is not far from the theatre. She has never had stage people before.

"You theatricals? Well, no fun an' games, like. This is a respectable establishment."

"Oh, no! We shall be far too tired for anything like that."

"Alright then. Twenty five shillings a week each, all in."

This sounds ridiculously cheap now, but we only got £8 to £12 per week pay, which had to cover costumes and travel as well as day to day living expenses and 10% to the agent.

Theatrical digs seem to have got an undeservedly bad reputation. We liked them. One got good meals; breakfast, lunch, a cup of tea and supper after the show; reasonable beds; a sitting room with a good fire. The family were very friendly and treated the artists as part of their own family. The only snag was the décor. You had to live with Great Aunt Hannah's glare from over the mantelpiece and Uncle Ernie leering from the sideboard but they were good for a laugh.

Well, *"Fraser & Chaytor"* have hardly settled in when it is evening and time to go to the theatre. We change, make up and go on stage and bag two chairs on which to arrange our quick changes – which are very quick indeed. Oh those changes!

It is de rigueur never to leave the stage empty so if you want to change from your first dance to the second, one of the dancers has to stay on stage and do some variations on dance number one while the other is changing for dance number two. The first dancer then goes off the change while the second begins to dance number two on her own. When you are offering three dances in a programme this is a bore. This has not really struck us before as we have been doing cabaret where our dances are sandwiched between other attractions. The other acts are critical.

"All that changing is no good, dear. You must tighten up your act."

"Nice dancing, dear, but all that mucking about spoils it."

We shall have to think of something.

The next day at the theatre there is a strange atmosphere of worry. People keep asking each other,

"Have you had your confirmation, dear? I haven't. I wonder why?"

"I haven't either. What shall we do about it?"

Rumours are going around.

"The managers are broke. They owe money all over town. Did you know the Hoover has been taken away and the gas turned off?"

We all wonder if we shall get paid. Those with heavy props to carry about, such as the roller skating act, are in a real state. Eventually the comic, who is top of the bill, goes to the office and comes back with all our confirmations. This is reassuring but we still worry. The front of house doorman – an enormous Yorkshireman – is very indignant about it all.

"Ee, I'll knock their damned blocks off if they don't give you girls your money. It's a reet shame."

On Saturday, before the show, there is a strike of the orchestra and stage staff. No pay – No play. Their salaries are all in arrears. After a lot of shouting the managers raid the bar till and pay the strikers in silver. The show goes on.

The stagehands are very worried about us and give us good advice.

"After the show change as quick as you can and get up to the office. Don't move until you are paid. They'll have enough money in the house now to pay everyone."

We follow their advice and find, not the manager, but a miserable little clerk in charge, who looks at the queue forming behind us and squeaks, "I can't pay you. I can't. I haven't any money!"

The queue begins to make threatening noises so he gives in and pays us. We hear later that some of the latecomers only got part of their money, so they raided the bar and took away armfuls of bottles.

What a start! But fortunately not the norm.

Now we move on to Wakefield where there is a nice, big theatre. We have been brooding over the matter of those changes. June has an idea.

"What about putting in a song?"

"All right, if you do the singing."

"Don't be daft! You know I can't sing two notes in tune. You must give it a try."

I let myself be persuaded and find a pop number in our pile of music. It is *I'm Young and Healthy and You've got Charm.* I sing this to the best of my ability but the manager comes round.

"You sing very nicely, dear, but you can't be heard beyond the second row of the stalls. Better stick to dancing."

I stick to dancing.

The manager is a very nice man. He seems to think we are an enormous joke. He invites us to parties in the bar to meet his friends and drives us all over the country in his car. He takes us to Redcar where we have a great walk on the beach. He is a really nice man.

CHAPTER IV
TWO REGULAR GUYS

We are back in London doing a lot of thinking about the act. Suddenly June remembers a scarecrow act she did in concert party.
"We could wear baggy scarecrow gear over our ballet costumes, that would be a novelty."
"With top hats and masks on the back of our heads we can do a backwards dance, which would be really funny."
"We can scrap the tap, do solos and finish with the novelty hornpipe."
We are pleased with our ideas and get busy. Printed feed sacks from June's grandfather's shop; old top hats; some hideous old man masks from Brixton make the scarecrows. For the ballet we have blue velvet bikinis studded with diamante and frilly, white organdie skirts. June does a Russian dance for her solo, for which she already has a costume and boots. I make up a polka dress for my act and we have various costumes for the hornpipe.
Now for the music. We buy a pile of big, stout music, cut up the band parts very carefully and stick in the right bits in the right order, clearly numbered. We are using *The Teddy Bear's Picnic, The Blue Danube, Russian Dance, See Me Dance the Polka* and *The Sailor's Hornpipe*. There is room in the books for other dances if, and when we make any up.

Our act has always been billed as *"June and Elaine"* as is usual with what are known as "sister acts". But as it is a new act, we want to be different. We want to be a surprise for people who will not know what, if anything is under those grotesque costumes – and will be amazed when two beautiful girls pop out! We therefore decide to call ourselves *"Two Regular Guys".* The act is no ordinary "sister act". The ballet is real ballet and in her solo bit, while I am changing for the polka, June does some terrific spins and entrachata. My solo is on point and endeavours to be coy. June's Russian dance is very good indeed as she does lots of cobblers (sitting down/kicking legs out bit), which always gets a lot of applause. In the solo hornpipe I do, while she is changing out of Russian dress, I do some conventional dance and then go into a series of fast cat-slings, which always gets a good hand, especially if the drummer will give me a roll. The hornpipe itself is pretty fast and breathless. Sometimes abroad we substitute a Scottish dance, in which my solo is the sword dance. Continentals like this, especially the very, very short kilts!

But now we head north again to the Alhambra in Bolton where we will try this act out. Our hard work has paid off! The new act works a treat! The scarecrow gear is effortlessly shed; we have just enough time for changes; the conductor is pleased with the band parts and the other acts approve.

"Nice little novelty act, dears, you should do alright."

Variety artists are a strange lot, always on the move, getting to know only each other and the various landladies who look after them. They travel everywhere but never see anything except the theatre, the digs, Woolworths and the pub. They have nothing to talk about except the awful state of the business. We found on the whole that acrobats are more fun, perhaps because they are so fit. They are very friendly and outgoing but often speak very little English. We sometimes work with some Hungarians. We can't really communicate but they like to come round to the digs for tea and buns and play gypsy music on a violin, which they seem to share.

Another amusing group are *The Gladiators*. They are midget acrobats, as strong as little tigers. Their manager is a huge man who strides onto the stage dressed, as are they all, as a gladiator, and produces the smallest midget from under his cloak. We have many a laugh together. When we meet they run over to us and we say,

"Now, Jacky, and Freddy, please shake hands gently. We don't want our mitts crushed again!"

The Four Aces, four lads from Stretham, are a lot of fun. They have a car and are very helpful with lifts. Another nice group are *The Four Paulettes,* Belgian acrobats – mother, father and two daughters. They have frightful quarrels in Flemish, a very strange language.

An act we do not bond with when we are on the same bill is *Stephan, The Armless Wonder.* He is a tall, thin, cross-looking man with long, thin legs, as graceful and supple as a ballet dancer's arms. He wears mittens on his feet in slip on shoes and can do anything with his toes: paint pictures; shoot a gun; knit; sew; and when in a pub, he lifts up his long, thin leg and holds his pint like anyone else. The theatre in Fleetwood where we are working, has a Saturday matinee. We all grumble but turn up – all that is except *The Armless Wonder* who has gone off somewhere. The kids in the audience are furious. They stamp and bang and yell,

"We want the 'armless man'! We want the 'armless man'!"

The poor manager is quite worried.

Another act we do not care for is *Wee Georgie Wood* who we think conceited and far too old for his little boy stunt.

What is under those grotesque scarecrow costumes?

People are amazed when two beautiful girls pop out!

Quite different from most pros is a harmony group of six very nice young men who seem like students – a bit like us. They go for walks, explore the countryside and even read books. One of them eventually became a well-known opera singer.

June's Russian dance – she does a lot of cobblers.

There was another famous person around at the time starting his career in rep. I found myself, years later, sitting next to Sir Laurence Olivier at a state banquet and we had quite a laugh comparing the awful dates we both had played.

My solo is on point and endeavours to be coy.

CHAPTER V

SUNDAYS AT CREWE

Quite a bit of work begins to come in which entails, of course, much travelling. Every town had its theatre, sometimes two or three. Most of these theatres changed their programmes weekly, so the artists were always on the move.
By train - On Sunday.

Most of these journeys are done by train. Very few pros can afford a car, which doesn't matter, as there are trains from everywhere. All you have to do is work out your route and your changes with a timetable, an essential item in anyone's luggage. Somehow, wherever you are going you sometime on that Sunday land at Crewe. Crewe appeared to be the lynchpin (whatever that may be) of the entire railway system.

> "Oh, Mr Porter what shall I do?
> They've set me down at Crewe!"

Everyone seems to be set down there. Pro calls to pro across the platforms.
"Glad to see you mate! Where you going?"
"Just done a week in Brixton and I'm off to Shotton."
"I played the Alhambra there last spring. Terrible business. Hi Joe! What's the news?"
The pros are cheerful while the rep companies stand in small groups with their luggage looking depressed.

For *Two Regular Guys* it is a different scene. We are *staying* in Crewe as we have a booking at the theatre. It is a dull, little town where we can't find anything to see or do. So when two of the local hicks turn up at the stage door to invite us out to dinner, we think,
"Well, why not go? They look pretty harmless."
They turn up with a car and drive us to a hotel on the outskirts of the town where we have quite a good dinner and some reasonably bright conversation − the best that can be worked up with our not very inspiring hosts. When we get to the coffee stage they asked to be excused for a moment. They have to make a phone call. It is a very long moment. We wait and wait. Presently the waiter comes along.
"Excuse me, ladies. The gentlemen 'as paid the bill an gone 'ome."

We can't believe it. We have been stood up by a pair of small town Romeos! We make our way home through the darkened streets. It takes us a long time as we have to keep stopping and leaning against the walls, we are laughing so much.

Of course, life is not all Crewe Station or featureless small towns. We have some dates in London, East Ham, West Ham and the Old Kent Road. We love working in the East End. The people are so nice. Going to work on the bus, you often find yourself holding someone's bundle or their baby and the stage hands are a comedy act in themselves.

Out of town the dates we like best are not the big cities with huge theatres, but seaside resorts or cathedral towns. The seaside is pretty quiet in winter. Their big effort is a resident concert party for three months in the summer. The rest of the year it is variety for the locals, who now have time to be friendly. It is lovely to take long walks by the sea.

At Prestatyn in North Wales we are by the sea but never see much of it. We hire two ancient bicycles we call Ferdinand and Isabella, on which we take long, daily rides through the beautiful surrounding countryside, often arriving back breathless with hardly time to make up and get on stage. It is here that a careless conjurer's assistant, doing her supporting act backstage, lets off a pistol so close to my ear that I am deaf for months.

Lincoln is a lovely town. The beautiful cathedral stands aloof on a surprisingly high hill, like an ecclesiastical Matterhorn. The little streets, which climb up to it, might well be in Italy. There is a splendid castle, too, where you can roam unattended and standing on the turret, see most of England spread out flatly before you.

York is a fascinating city. Staying for a week there is time to get to know the quaint little streets where the upper stories of the houses lean out so much they nearly collide, the grand Minster with its close and to take long walks round the walls which nearly encircle it.

Chester is also a good place from which to get out to see some beautiful country. The cathedral is red sandstone and here there are also some good city walls.

Sometimes we stay at June's home in Manchester for a few weeks. She knows all the local agents who fix up quite a lot of work for us round and about. Living at home for a bit makes a nice change. We cook endless eggs and chips and do mounds of washing. June's parents and grandfather share the house. He is a nice old Scottish gent whose hobby is racing pigeons. He has two yappy little pug dogs. June's mother also has two yappy pugs and a parrot, which has learnt to bark, and does. You sometimes need earplugs in June's home!

CHAPTER VI

A TOUCH OF THE BLARNEY

Early in the summer an interesting engagement comes up. It is for three weeks in Ireland – Dublin, Belfast and Cork with *Archie's Juvenile Band*. Well, here we are on the overnight ferry from Holyhead steaming into Cobh at a very early hour indeed. We take a bus into Dublin. Now to find our digs. There are not many people about but we stop someone to ask for directions. He is friendly and helpful.

"Gabble, gabble, gabble," he says.

We can't understand a word but thank him and go on and try another, with the same result – and another, and another. We might as well be in Vladivostok! The day wears on and we get more tired and more hungry. Then we see a man in a bowler hat with a briefcase and him we *can* understand.

Dublin is a nice, friendly city. Somehow it seems to be both big and small at the same time. We walk by the Liffey and are taken to some catacombs which contain corpses naturally mummified by the local conditions.

Now we are off to Belfast, where we encounter our first irishism when we ask the way.

"Ye'll not miss it. Tis the second on the left, not counting the first."

Belfast city is not a great deal of fun, but the local hospitality is quite something. June's mother has alerted some old friends of our arrival. They come to see the show and subsequently take us for many drives around and about the area. We see lakes, the Mountains of Mourne, Bangor and many other places. There are lunches and splendid Irish teas with scones, cakes and soda bread.

Hospitality is pretty strong in the theatre, too. There is a bar in the stalls down in the prompt corner, which has an opening onto the stage itself. Drinks are continually sent up to us by appreciative members of the audience. Were it not for the helpfulness of the stage staff in disposing of them, we should be dancing flat on our backs.

That week has finished and we are all on the night train to Cork, hoping to get some sleep. One of the acts, a male and female singing duo, who have the compartment next to ours, are in the middle of a major row. It seems that she has borrowed his umbrella and lost it. We can't really hear the words for the shouting, but now and again the same complaint is heard – continuo, fortissimo.

"*. . . . and* a bloody Foxframe!"
We bang on the partition and shout,
"Shut up! Shut up!" but nothing stops them. Then we have our revenge in Cork.

The Juvenile Band are a great lot of kids, real troupers. When we find they have digs over the umbrella people, we ask them to stamp and tap dance at inconvenient times.

The opera house in Cork is impressive but rather scruffy. Over the years stage cloths have been nailed down and subsequently ripped up leaving a shiny strip of nail-heads, quite dangerous to dance on. Our costumes, even our most sober ones, are deemed too revealing. We have to wear blouses under them. The manager here is very nice and jolly. He takes us for drives to show us the local beauty spots. We see the lakes of Killarney, mountains and lovely sandy beaches. Most of the juvenile band go off to see the Blarney Stone. The local transport, not being very time conscious, lets them down. They miss their opening but this does not phase the head boy. He gathers together what instrumentalists he has got and they start off bravely playing. As they return, the missing players slide unobtrusively into their places and carry on with no fuss. A very sound lot.

The theatre electrician, Cork Opera House, 1934.

27

CHAPTER VII
SAMSON AND CO.

Back in England we have three dates booked with a little show run by *Samson the Strong Man* act. Various well meaning people warn us about him.

"You'll have to look out. I hear he's a real devil with the ladies!"

We set off from Lincoln, the first date, with some trepidation. This increases when we get to the digs, some very good ones kept by a retired butler and his wife, to find Samson and his wife also staying there. He appears at once, a short, homely, thickset man in a bowler hat.

"Hello, boys! You mit me?"

Samson was a type probably usual in the circuses where he had worked but most unusual on the variety circuit. Far from being a lothario, he was a quiet, friendly man who loved to collect a few friends after the show, sit around the fire with a bottle of chianti and tell stories. His own, as told in his fractured English, is well worth recording. He came from Turkestan.

"Mine fader, he have six wife, mine uncle eight. I vewy strong boy. I plough, I fight, I much ride. Fifty miles one night to see my girl friend, fifty back. Come on boys! What you have? More one drink and we make party good! Now, what I tell you? Those was good times. Good land, much grass, many cattles. I ride good horses, make much wrestling, love beautiful girls. Then come war. I Cossack officer. End of war I white Russian and run to Hungary, to Budapest. Bad times then. I no work, no eat, no drink. Every day make belt more tight. Then I find circus. First I clean horses; then I wrestle; then I make dog act very good. Then have good agent. Make big strong man act. Much, much money; much travel; go every place. Now agent dead and I think strong man finish."

Poor Samson, he was such an honest, simple soul. After his agent died, his wife ran away with his money and people cheated him right and left.

There are several acts we know in this outfit. *Les Four Paulettes*, a contortionist and Jack Martell, a comedy juggler with us make up the variety half, the rest being Samson's show – mainly his strong man stuff. He has a lot of amazingly heavy props. There are chains to break, sheets of metal to tear, a cannon which shoots a big, steel ball he catches on his chest and a huge girder which he lifts with first with two fingers and then with his teeth. Would-be strong men who come up from the audience cannot lift it at all. He used to hang by one foot from the flies holding in his teeth a platform on which sat a lady playing the piano. Since his wife left he doesn't do that, or some very spectacular stunts with horses and wagon,

Samson.

which are strictly for the circus. There are also his animal acts. Samson is wonderful with animals and they seem to love to do tricks for him.

First is Polly, the pony. He ends his act by carrying her round the stage. She is a fat little 13'2" and no light weight. She has been in a circus and does tricks. She can count to ten, shake hands, say 'thankyou' and walk on her hind legs. There are some very jolly dogs and some quite awful monkeys – Toby, Betty, Cheerful, Dismal and Happy. Toby is old and cross and has to be kept on a lead. He goes to the pub with Samson and drinks his beer like a man. Betty has baby Happy clinging to her like a little frog.. Dismal is just a nuisance. He climbs up the tabs, gets in the orchestra, pulls the music about and throws things at the audience. Cheerful helps him if he can slip away. So here are *Fraser and Chaytor*, alias *Two Regular Guys,* in the circus – well, sort of – and having a lot of fun.

The week at Lincoln goes well. It is a nice theatre, the houses are good, and we introduce everyone to the ice cream shop.

Next is Bradford, a big, noisy city with a large, smart theatre. The stage manager is not happy to have monkeys all over the place, climbing his beautiful, blue tabs. The following week we move on to Nelson, but what a calamity! This is a small town we have never heard of. There is a lot of unemployment and people look depressed – so do we when we see our place of work. There are two theatres. Samson, with no agent to guide him, has got lumbered with the smaller one, which is tiny. By the time all the huge props have been dragged in, there is only half a small stage for everyone to work on. The dressing rooms are in a semi-derelict hut next door, the orchestra just a piano and a violin. Business the first night is so poor we decide we must do something to help, so we consult Albert.

Albert is groom, van driver and helper in general. He is a great fellow with ginger hair, two teeth, a terrific cockney accent and an endless fund of stories about the circuses in which he seems to have spent his life. We like him. He is so fond of, and kind to the animals. He had an endless store of anecdotes, many about the animals of which he was so fond. He assured us that no animal will hurt a drunk.

One night the bear keeper got very drunk, so when he got back to the circus and couldn't find his caravan, he got in the bears' cage and went to sleep with them. These were very cross bears, however, so when he woke up and realised where he was, he had to lie perfectly still until the other keepers saw him and brought poles to hold the bears back.

A man did a very dangerous looking act with a lion in a bedroom set. He comes home from an evening out to find the lion in his bed so they do all sorts of tricks together. He has no stick or whip but pretends to be very drunk the whole time.

Samson was travelling with Toby, his very bad tempered monkey who bit everybody. One day he tied Toby up in the carriage while he went out for a short while. When he got back he found a drunken sailor had untied the monkey and they were asleep in a corner with their arms round each other. He had to exercise much tact to get them apart.

In another circus where they had a sea lion act, the little daughter of the ringmaster used regularly to escape from her mother, climb into the sea lion enclosure and sit with her arms round the neck of the big male saying, "Dear doggie! Dear doggie!"

We do love listening to Albert's stories but now we have a job to do and need Albert's help to turn around the fortunes of Samson's company. With his help we make the caravan gay with flags, balloons and ourselves dress up in gypsy gear. We drive around the town giving out some leaflets Samson had produced to promote the show. Our efforts work because the houses become much better.

It is early summer with lovely weather and beautiful country nearby. Samson decrees we should all have a day out so when Albert has loaded the animals and us in the caravan, we set off for the moors, where a wonderful time is had by all. The dogs chase rabbits, the pony rolls and grazes, the monkeys find a little stream which is great for watery games and we take a long walk up the hills and then lie in the heather for a rest. Everyone is so full of fresh air and exercise it is hard to work that night. The dogs are far too excited.

We are all going back to London so Samson offers to give us a lift in the caravan. Luckily *Les Paulettes* have gone elsewhere as there is very little room, with all Samson's props, the pony's stall and the dogs and monkeys in cages. Samson, Albert and the contortionist are up in front in the driving cab. In the dim interior June has to lie on the monkeys' cage. They spend all night trying to pinch her. Elaine beds down by the pony, who spends the night searching her pockets for cake. Jack Martell and the comic crouch in a corner complaining loudly and rudely about the atmosphere. Samson must have lost money on that venture but he never lost heart. We used to run into him sometimes in London.

"You alright, boys? You got work? You plenty eat? Come to my house, we have bottle chianti, make party? Yes?"

He ended his life as head keeper at Paignton Zoo, where he must have been very happy.

CHAPTER VIII

ON THE ROAD

We get a short break in town before heading north again. We are getting very tired of trains. Suddenly June has an idea.

"Why don't we buy a car and save all this bother?"

"Well, we can't drive."

"It can't be all that difficult. We'll soon learn."

We read the small ads in the local paper, see one that sounds possible and get the friendly theatre manager to drive us out to this farm to see it. The car is a Morris, one of the very first square nosed models they made after giving up the old bull nose. It looks a bit dilapidated, as does the shed in which it lives, as also, come to think of it does the whole place. The manager drives round the field a bit, says it seems to go all right. The price is right too – it is only £10 – so we buy it, go back to town, fix up a cover note (again the helpful manager) and buy driving licences. Next day we go out to the farm for a driving lesson round and round the field. We find reversing difficult. The car goes well, but it is hard to stop. The rest of the week we spend practising our driving round the lanes.

One day June drives down a lane, turns into a road rather fast, when CRASH! A speedy cycle hurtles into the side of our car smashing the toolbox. Cars in those days had running boards alongside, on which was a little doormat to wipe your feet and a wooden box full of tools. The cyclist has demolished this so we are angry. He is cross about his bent wheel. We exchange addresses and part. We decide to put the bits of box together so it looks all right when we go on. Presently the car starts to make a funny noise so we pull into a garage. The kindly owner says, yes, he will look into the funny noise so gets in the car. Crash! Again! He has stepped on the broken box and it is now in smithereens.

"Oh dear! I am sorry, how terribly careless of me. If you are not in a hurry, I will fix you up with a new tool box."

We are not and he does.

Eventually we have to pay the cost of the bent wheel. We tell this story to the solicitor who thinks it is so funny he calls in his partner so he can have a laugh too.

Our next engagement is four weeks at the Beach Pavilion, Aberdeen, with Harry Gordon's Concert Party. This is a very, very long drive but we manage it somehow. We are very glad we have the car, as the Beach Pavilion is quite a long way from the town and our digs.

With Harry Gordon's Concert Party in Aberdeen.

Harry Gordon turns out to be a nice old boy with an impenetrable Scottish accent. He has ten permanent members of his company, enlivening their efforts with new dances every four weeks. In the first week we do our act but spend all day rehearsing sketches for the following week's show. They seem to think that I can act, as I am in many sketches and have a lot of lines to learn. Costumes are provided by wardrobe.

The second week our contribution is a shepherdess number on point. I have the star part in a comic verse sketch built on "Daisy, Daisy", in which I wear my false curls on the front of my head, instead of the back, a conceit much admired. Harry Gordon can never remember his lines so I prompt him in a whisper. He gets a good laugh by saying loudly,

"A ken the noo."

The third week we do an Isadora number in green bikinis with long, yellow and green scarves, which we wave about. I have a sketch in which I come on ostensibly to sing a song but after two bars, clutch my throat and fall with a crash to the floor. The on stage pianist rushes to help me calling out,

"Is there a doctor in the house?"

Noises from the back of the stalls turn out to be the two comics, Harry Gordon and friend, dressed as ambulance men, who try to revive my inanimate body with much Scottish humour.

The last week we offer an item, which we have never had time properly to rehearse. I am a mermaid sitting on a property rock. June is an amorous codfish. She has a grey tailcoat, a grey top hat and a fish mask. She is so keen on this outfit that she gets the electrician to fix up two shining eyes in the mask with a battery in the hat to work them. She wasn't far into the dance when this affair started. She ran round and round the stage screaming, tearing at the immovable hat, until someone rescued her. The dance was intended to be amusing but not like that!

At the end of our engagement with Harry Gordon we are heading south to Birkenhead. The length of the drive decides us to start the night before so, late on Saturday, after a farewell party, we set off. After a while the headlights pass out. We decide to park in a lay-by and wait for dawn. By the lay-by is a dark wood. June, who is psychic, is unhappy.

"We can't possibly stay here. It is haunted. It is horrible!"

I didn't like it much myself so we press on arriving a Birkenhead late at night and absolutely knackered.

June is staying with friends but I have some really bad digs. Some relation of the landlady's has died somewhere, not in the house. She insists on having all the blinds down all the time so I have to live in the dark. The theatre is not much fun either, being in a very rough district. We are told that if we are not liked, the audience will throw things.

On Saturday night the stage boxes are crammed with large lads with crates of beer. We fear the worst but, though they rough up some of the later performers, we get nothing worse than some lascivious shouting.

We spend the following week resting in June's home with her nice mum, the dogs and the parrot.

The fish and the mermaid.

CHAPTER IX

OVERSEAS

Bookings have been falling off a bit so when an agent says he can fix us up with four weeks' cabaret in Belgium, we are delighted but slightly apprehensive. You meet some pretty odd people in the business but you learn to cope with them. It is a great help being two when it comes to managing an awkward situation. What will these foreign cabarets be like? We do not know at this time that English dancers abroad have the reputation of being so straight laced that predatory characters shy away.

Our empty diaries make us decide to risk it, so taking the night ferry to Antwerp and a train to Ghent, we find our way to the small, shabby hotel into which the agent has booked us. The comfortable digs of the English circuit are unknown on the continental round. Artists stay in hotels whose grade is equated with their earning level, and take their meals out.

Ghent is a pretty little town. There are big, Dutch looking houses along the many canals with lots of little bridges and much water traffic. Along the banks are many street markets. As we do not like to go out for so many meals, we buy a meta stove, some plates, cups, spoons and forks, also some food. We can at least make our own breakfast.

Now it is off with our gear to find the den of vice to which we have enslaved ourselves. The address given turns out to be a large, modern building with the cabaret, to our surprise, on the first floor. It is no sinister dive but a large, bright room like a restaurant with a dance floor, nice dressing rooms, a good little band and a friendly manager. The place fills up slowly with respectable looking couples and family parties. The maitre tells us we are on so we do our first show.

"Very nice. Very good." He says, thrusting a small wooden bowl into my hands. We are surprised and puzzled.

"Now you must do a quête. You must go round to all the people. They will give you money which you will put in that little box by the band, the one with your name on it."

We are horrified. What? Go begging for tips? Not us!

"Oh, but you must. It is the custom, here. The money you collect you will share with the band at the end of the evening. If you do not do this they will play your music badly and spoil your act."

June is very upset.

"I can't! I can't possible do such a thing," she wails.

"This is not our scene, but we are not at home now. We must do what the people who have hired us expect, without fuss."

I take round the bowl. People throw in a few coins which I duly tip into the little box, feeling quite a heroine!

We have a very long wait before our second performance, so we sit in a corner to watch the other acts. It appears that this is quite an up-market place, which does not expect the artists to sit with the customers between shows – apparently de rigueur in the sleazier establishments.

Our two weeks up, we find ourselves in Brussels booked in at The Parisienne, which seems to be a very smart and expensive looking night club. There are twelve entraineuse, or hostesses, two gigolos, a good-sized band and an impressive doorman. We find all that is expected of us is two shows. There is no quête and no compulsory sitting with the customers. However, there is a long, long interval between our two performances so eventually we decide it is less boring to change and sit at an unobtrusive table near the band. We meet people, mostly quite amusing yuppie types or foreigners tired of trying to be jolly with minimal French. The entraineuses' job is to amuse people, persuade them to buy champagne (very expensive) and give them a big tip. If they go home with any of their customers, it is done very discreetly. The young men who come know we are not on the make so we have some very jolly evenings.

A cabaret in the early evening, before anybody has come, is a strange sight. The lights are dim, the girls and boys are quietly chatting, the band lounge about smoking. Then the doorman buzzes. Instant party! The band is in the middle of a number. The boys and girls are dancing together. Waiters rush about. There is light. Sometimes this is a false alarm and instant torpor again prevails.

When in Brussels, we always stay at the Hotel Post, a small, old fashioned place but conveniently central and cheap. One day there is nearly a catastrophe. We have two spirit lamps now, on which we are making our breakfast, on the broad windowsill. There are several layers of curtains in these old places and flames begin to lick up them in a very alarming way. We are not dressed for fire fighting - in fact we are not dressed at all. I call to June who is at the wash-basin.

"Soak the towels and throw them across to me!"

I bang at the flames with the wet towels and manage to put the fire out. What a mess is left – burnt curtain, burnt windowsill!

"Goodness, what a mess. What will madam say?"

"We must make it good as quickly as possible."

Top priority is the curtain. Our room is on the corner and has three windows, each with three layers of curtains, two of them muslin, so we replace the burnt one with a similar sort from the furthest one. The burnt bits we will deposit in The Parisienne's bin. Then there is the windowsill.

"We'll get some white paint to cover up the mess."

"That will smell, and give her ideas."

"If we re-paint our white tap shoes, the old ones, that will account for any smell."

This we do. It must have worked as she never said anything or sued us for enormous damages.

While at The Parisienne we are approached by some local agents, Krebs and Liberman, who offered us a date in Antwerp, at The Globe.

"It is not a grand place but the money is good. If Madame likes you she will keep you on for a long time."

Dear little Krebs and Liberman. We worked for them for months and months without any contract or written agreement. We always got our money and of course delivered the goods. I hope they did not perish in the Holocaust.

Antwerp, we find, is not at all like Brussels. It is Flemish, much more relaxed and jolly than the rather formal, frenchified style of the capital city. We find The Globe and are rather horrified. A long passage, which is also a bar, leads into a smallish dance room with no sign of dressing rooms, which turn out to be upstairs.

"We can't work here," says June. "It is too small, too dark and too horrible. It looks like a pub."

"We're contracted for two weeks so we shall just have to put up with it and hope our next date will be better."

We rehearse, glad to find the band is so good and do our act, luckily without hitting or breaking anything. Madam comes up to the dressing room. She likes our act but would prefer us to do separate dances, which suits us well.

The set up at The Globe is totally different from The Parisienne, and much more down-market. We have to sit with the customers and do the quête. No champagne appears but beer, whiskey and short drinks. The clients match the drinks. There are students, medical and otherwise, young doctors and business men, rugby players, all very jolly and noisy. We are asked to join their parties and make a lot of friends. The club is always full and stays open for hours and hours. We make so many friends that Madam asks us to stay on indefinitely. The late hours are tiring but with the wages, the quête and the cut we get on hard drinks, the money is good. The drinking would be a problem were it not for an arrangement we make with the sardonic English barman. He fixes the drinks bought for us by the customers so they look all right but have a very low alcohol content.

We live in a little hotel quite near the club and have a lovely, big, attic room with windows looking over a sea of roofs and chimney pots, just like

The Met's set for La Bohème. We are the only people actually living in this building. All the other rooms are let out by the hour for sex sessions. This makes for embarrassing encounters when you bump into one of your friends coming in with a lady.

Our friends are almost too good at taking us out at the weekend because that is when we make up on a bit of sleep. Still, they are very kind. One very rich young man, son of Philips Electrics, takes us both out for an enormous and much appreciated lunch, before going off with June for the rest of the day.

The weeks roll on and suddenly it is Christmas. We walk around the market full of the nostalgic scent of Christmas trees. Then, before work, we have a little party with two German girl acrobats who are also at The Globe. We pool our food and drink and sing carols in two languages.

Early one evening when we are just getting dressed and made up, Madame comes in, in a great state.

"There is a English boxer in the town. He has just won a big match. They say he is loaded with money and quite drunk and coming HERE! I'm sure he will break the place up. Please will you go and try to get him away?"

"Well, we'll do what we can to help, Madame, but we may not be able to do much."

"You can have the whole evening off, if you will only try."

When we get down to the bar the boxer and his minder are already there. He is huge, he is drunk and he has wads of money sticking out of every pocket. We go up to him.

"Congratulations on your win. Are you having a good time?"

He looks very aggressive.

"Too many girls, young girls. Doan wan' girls. Girls wan' my money. Ish my money. Not goin' have my money."

"We don't want your money. We're English. We have lots of money of our own."

"Aw right, not take my money. Letch 'ave a drink."

He bangs his huge fist on the bar and yells, "Drinks!"

Madame is flapping her hands is the background, looking more and more agitated.

"This is an awful place – bad drinks. Let's go somewhere nice and have some drinks and dinner."

"Yesh! All go drink. No have my money."

"No, no. No-one's going to touch your money. Come on."

We lead him out. He is pretty unsteady so we walk one each side of him like two little tugs escorting a liner. His minder seems to have vanished into the night.

"Let's go to your hotel for a drink and some dinner."

"Yesh. Wan' a drink. You wan' drink. Lotsh, lotsch of drink. Go to hotel."
We assumed he would be staying at The Palace, so we wove a slightly
wobbly path to that establishment and sat him down on a settee in the
lounge.
"Now, you order lots of drinks. We are going to the ladies room."
We scoot off through the pass door, find a helpful waiter who shows us the
back way out and we are soon home.

Brussels Exposition, 1935 – entrance.

Brussels, 1935.

CHAPTER X

SAUSAGE, SAUSAGE, SAUSAGE!

By the turn of the year we begin to feel like a change, so when Krebs and Liberman come round to pay us, we ask them to find us some other jobs. As a result of this we find ourselves in Liège, in the north east of Belgium. This is a dull little manufacturing town with nothing, as far as we can see, to do. The only thing of interest is a very good little milliner who makes us some nice felt hats. They are quite inexpensive because she makes a cut for theatricals. We always wear hats except on holiday so we are glad to stock up.

After Liege it is back to Brussels to The Hungarica. There is little of Hungary about this club except the doorman's uniform and a gypsy violinist. Then on to The Kasak, which is slightly more ethnic. We feel we owe Brussels something fresh, so we put on two new numbers; a Hawaiian and a rhumba with some eye-catching costumes.

An interesting booking follows, not in Belgium but in Luxembourg, at The Pole Nord Hotel. We are quite excited at going to a new country and one, too, which is something quite out of the ordinary. It is very hilly and wooded with terrific gorges spanned by dizzy looking bridges running through the town. We find The Pole Nord to have a big restaurant with a dance floor, not looking at all like a night-club, which it certainly isn't. The only other act is *The Five Melodisten*, a group of large, silent, young Germans who sing in harmony. We are all lodged and boarded in the hotel, which is fine, except that meals are terribly monotonous. We can put up with this but the singers cannot. After four days they begin banging on the table at lunch and continue until the manager comes.

"We will not go on so," says the one who speaks English, "It is sausage, sausage, sausage! Every day is more sausage. Is black sausage, red sausage, brown sausage, white sausage. More sausage we will not have!"

After that the meals did improve a bit.

There are not many customers at the first dinner dance but a young man, who has been sitting in a corner with a beer, comes round after the show to speak to us. He is Steven Williams, who was at school with my brothers. He is in charge of Radio Luxemburg, the commercial station, which is housed in part of a beautiful, old castle. Steven gives us the freedom of the studio, so we spend many happy hours there, sitting drinking coffee in the sunny courtyard, Steven dashing into the studio just in time to do his talk and change the record.

We now decide it is about time to go back to England, see our families and make some new sets of costumes, ours having got very shabby. We find the variety scene has changed. Instead of booking eight separate acts, the agents and managers have devised a scheme, which will provide the same amount of entertainment at less cost. They are booking about five acts, which have to do sketches and combined numbers. Variety has become a kind of cut-price review and we do not fancy it.

We now have digs in Gower Street, which is gloomy but central, a must, as we are now existing on cabaret engagements. We work one-week stands at The Monico, The Connaught Rooms, The Hammersmith Palais and others. There are also one-night stands where some private party or other wishes entertainment. These are as amusing as ever. The dressing rooms are anywhere – in a pantry or a passage, often near the kitchen. The waiters are hurried but friendly and we get many a delicious snack. At The Savoy a dear old waiter wraps up a big pile of sandwiches in a Savoy serviette and gives them to me, saying,

"Go on. You take them. You girls never has enough to eat!"

We have a good laugh this evening. There are several other acts, one a strong lady who hurls her little husband around in a highly comical manner. When a mouse runs across the room, she shrieks loudly and jumps on a chair.

A strange date is at The Thatched Barn Restaurant in Barnet on the A1. The management drive us out there in a minibus to entertain the diners, then drive us back to Soho, where they have a night club in which we have to perform to a rather drunk audience at a very late hour. We find all the travelling a bit much – but worse is to come.

Some theatres, which had converted to cinemas, are not doing the business they expected so they decide to hire a few acts to jolly up the evening. They own two cinemas but can only afford one copy of the big picture, the B picture and the cartoon. Everything and everyone has to travel between the two houses. Imagine the complications: The Hackney Empire is giving three shows and The Mile End Alhambra two. We start at Hackney with the B picture, the cartoon and the acts. While the big picture is playing, we scramble into a bus, clutching our impedimenta, to drive to Mile End. The Under Manager also scrambles in clutching the films of the B picture and cartoon. So the evening goes on – back and forth, back and forth. It is hard to remember what show you are doing, where. The travelling is not made easier by the fact that the other act on the bill is *Evelyn Hardy's Ladies Band*, who have to manage this busing with instruments, music and stands. The actual dancing is not much fun either as the stage is very polished and slippery with no floats to show where the edge is. The lighting is a blinding spot from the projection room; the music provided in a very strange manner by the mighty Wurlitzer's organist, who likes to let himself go.

People on the Continent liked the very short kilts worn in the Scottish Dance.

Sometimes we have a cabaret after all this, in the West End. We are working in one such when a message comes round. A Mr Simon would like to see us. Now this is a very well known character, who puts on lavish concert parties and shows. He asks us to join him.

"I've a show coming on at the North Pier, Blackpool. I want you two in it." He has a little dogsbody with him who doesn't like this at all.

"But, Mr Simon. You know we have already engaged all the artists we need. We simply don't want any more."

"I want this act and I want it fitted in. Are you two free next week for rehearsals? Good! Give them a promissory note, Sam. We'll see about a contract next week."

Sam writes the note then and there. It gives the date for the start of rehearsals and the pay. He doesn't look very happy about it. Mr S. is still full of enthusiasm, so we thank him and go home.

"I don't think that note is valid as a contract." I tell June, "We have one or two dates lined up. Let's stick to them and call this thing off."

"Oh, no! It will be a run of several months and quite near my home," said June, "We must go."

She is so keen that we cancel the possibilities and set off for Blackpool.

What a place! No one has any idea of the horror unless they have been there in Wakes Week, and it always seems to be Wakes Week. Streets, trams, buses, shops, arcades are all crammed with happy, friendly, outgoing people eating fast food, drinking out of cans or bottles and all wanting you to join their party. I can't imagine surviving here for three months. The North Pier is reasonably quiet and in the big theatre the rehearsal is underway. We are sent to Wardrobe to be measured for opening and finale costumes. We see the conductor, are given a timetable and eventually run through our show.

Next day is the first dress rehearsal, which goes on and on and on. It is obvious that some things will have to be cut and we wonder which will be the item to be sacrificed. Arriving for the final dress rehearsal we see a provisional programme pinned up. We are not on it. *We* are cut! Sam comes over to say how sorry they are and gives us two weeks wages. June is very upset. She cries and says we must *do* something.

"We'll take Mr Simon to court and sue him for a whole summer's earnings."

"We should look pretty silly if we did that. The note Sam gave us is not a proper contract. We haven't a leg to stand on."

"Well, what are we going to do? If we go back to town everyone will be laughing at us."

"There is only one thing to do. Ring up Krebs and Liberman." So we do.

CHAPTER XI

BRUSSELS TO BUDAPEST AND BELGRADE

Krebs and Lieberman are most helpful. Yes, they have work. We can start next Sunday in a cabaret in the amusement park of The Exposition International. (It is at this point that we decide to sell the car.) Of course we have heard of this huge exhibition as preparations for it have been going on in Brussels for several years. We certainly never expected to work in it. Here we are though, back at the Hotel Post and off with our props and music to find our place of work, El Mexicano, which is in the middle of a street of temporary restaurants and cabarets. This is bounded on one side by dodgems, roundabouts and white knuckle rides and on the other by stalls and shies of every description, all very noisy. The proprietors of our place have obviously made an effort. Straw hats and ponchos adorn the walls and the band wear bright, silk shirts but there is a very un-Mexican lethargy about the place and business is poor.

"Shall we suggest brightening things up a bit, like we did for Samson?"

"Why not? We've nothing to do between shows."

The manager is delighted when we take straw hats and ponchos from the wall decorations and stand outside shouting our wares in French and Spanish. It makes quite a difference as people now begin to come in. They must be a bit surprised at the extremely European entertainment, which, apart from us, consists of a Balkan type singer and a pair of coloured tap dancers from London's East End, a most amusing couple of real born and bred cockneys. Bob, the male dancer, doesn't care a hoot about foreign cabaret managers. After we have all done several shows he says,

"It's bloomin' late. We done enough, I'm orf 'ome."

So we all beat it without asking permission.

After the Exposition we are off to the seaside with dates at Knocke, La Zaite and Blankenberg. We manage to rent a tiny flat in Knocke with a proper kitchen. It is so nice, we decide to stay there during engagements and get to work by bicycle.

The Belgian coast is very boring – just miles of sand backed by beach huts, hotels and casinos but it is very good cycling country. We go along quite early to whichever town we are working in, have a good day on the beach and pedal home just as dawn is breaking. We often pause on a bridge for a joke or two with the English sailors on the night ferry, which comes in about then.

It is in Blankenberg that we make friends with a Hungarian couple, adagio dancers. They are very impressed with our act. Imré says,
"If you would like to go to Budapest I can easily book you in a big cabaret there. The manager is an old friend of mine. I think you will be a big success."
If we would like? What a question!
Imré gets busy on the phone and we find ourselves booked for a month at The Roseland Cabaret, as from the end of our seaside dates.

On the beach at Blankenberg.

Well, here we are on the night train to Budapest feeling slightly apprehensive. Imré has assured us that we will easily get other bookings at the end of our month but we are glad to feel we have enough money to pay our fare back in case things don't work out. The journey is long and the seats very hard. We hope there will be an English speaking person to meet us. All is well. The agent's clerk is waiting for us and he takes us to a hotel to wait while he fixes up our room. We wish to go to the Ladies' room in the foyer but which is the Ladies? The doors are labelled 'FERFI' and 'NOK' but which are we? The only solution to this problem is to wait. Eventually along comes what proves to be a Nok, so we are Ferfi.

We have a rather gloomy room on the eighth floor of a house in Kivali Utica, or King Street. It has a tiny balcony on which you can just stand but I never do as I get such a terrible feeling of fear. (I learn many years later that during the Nazi occupation, young Jewish girls used to jump off these balconies with their babies rather than be taken to the labour camps.)

Our room is an easy walk to the cabaret which is large, elegant and has roses everywhere − artificial ones in the dance room but real ones in tubs on a big, open balcony which is an open air restaurant.

The clientele are largely the Beautiful People who come to dance. Hungarians love dancing, especially a ballroom version of the Czardas. Some of the clients are men on the lookout for girls. This is our first experience of the Eastern Europe fashion for "Separes". These are little rooms below the main dance room where men invite girls to join them for an evening of drink and sex. The girls who sing and dance in the floor-show do their turn with this in mind. Very often at the end of the evening, there is only Fraser and Chaytor left in the ballroom, chatting to the barman.

The Roseland is a good place to dance but the dressing room is awful, small and packed with girls who make fun of us in Hungarian. We make an awful fuss and are given a dungeon, or something like it, below. Here we can spread out a bit, though someone sneaks in and steals our chocolates.

Budapest is a lovely city in which to spend a summer month. We walk by the Danube, which is dirty grey, or climb up the steep bluff on which stands the old castle and many spectacular old buildings. In the middle of the river is a big island, which has been made into a sports complex. The swimming pool is a great attraction and we go there every day. Barrow boys sell boiled sweet corn cobs.

We only meet one Hungarian socially. He is an elderly man who we think must be lonely. He buys us a drink one evening and says he would like to drive us round the city to show us the sights. When we meet him the following day, he gives us each a brightly coloured umbrella, so of course we call him the "Umbrella Man". He does indeed drive us all over the city to see everything of interest, takes us out to tea many times and buys us embroidered blouses and flowers in great quantity.

June has made friends with a young dentist who asks us to go on the river with him one Sunday. Loaded with bathing things and bags of food, we arrive at the boat shed. Everywhere there are the Beautiful People, immaculately turned out in white, stepping into slim, shining racing skiffs. There is our host, standing beside one of these vessels. He looks a bit aghast at our bundles, obviously not the correct thing, but fits us all in.

"You can row first," he says, "I'll take over later."

"We don't know how to row. We've never tried."

"It's quite easy. You'll soon manage."

Easy it is not. The boat is wobbly. There are two sliding seats and each of us has two oars. The Beautiful People slide smoothly and swiftly past. They are too grand to laugh at our erratic strokes and continual crabs. Pretty soon our host says he will take over and rows us swiftly up stream to one of the little sandy islands in the middle of the Danube. We spend a very pleasant day among the willows, the aspens and the many flowers. Anyone who wants to swim walks to the sandy beach at the tip of the island and swims back with the current feeling like an Olympic gold medallist. At dusk everyone paddles quietly home, some of them singing.

A day on the Danube.

Imré had been right about the availability of work. The agent booked us on the Zagreb, Belgrade, Bucharest and Sofia, so we are soon off on our travels again. Working abroad has one great disadvantage; there is no Sunday free for travelling. You finish work late on Saturday or early Sunday morning, pack, catch a night train, arrive at your next spot on Monday, rehearse and perform, having had what sleep is possible in a hard third class carriage. To make these journeys as bearable as possible, we tour a small suitcase, which is our commissariat. The dismal, grey dawn on these trips depresses the hardiest spirits but while other passengers are gloomily wondering if there will be a stop where they can get coffee, we open our case, set up our meta stove, make a cup of tea and have our breakfast.

Zagreb proves to be a dull town with little to see. The few locals we meet seem rather a rough lot but two nice Czechs, who were there on business, take us out to lunch and are very jolly. A strange sight in the town are the flocks of geese and turkeys looked after by old peasant women. Any housewife can go and choose her dinner, which would be slaughtered on the spot.

Zagreb is really very western but not so our next stop in Belgrade. It is built on a high knoll overlooking the junction of the Danube and the Sava with views over miles and miles of plains. On the highest point is an interesting old fort with pleasant gardens in and around it – the municipal park. Here, in the evenings, groups of giggling girls walk up and down, watched by hopeful bands of young men. There must be a strict code of behaviour as one never saw them fraternising. The girls all wear a very attractive local costume – an embroidered blouse and waistcoat top, an extremely full skirt which seems to consist of layer upon layer of brightly coloured petticoats, so many it sticks out like a ballet tutu. If this poem has got its facts right they must have scores of admirers.

> "A little pink petty from Peter,
> A little blue petty from Paul,
> And one green and yellow
> From some other fellow
> Whose name I just cannot recall."

The Serbs do not seem to be a dancing race but a lot of them enjoy our show, invite us to their table for a drink and subsequently take us out for long drives to show us the country of which they are extremely proud, and rightly. It is quite mountainous with beautiful lakes and woods – a bit like Scotland. Our hosts are plain, straightforward, friendly people and we like them very much. We both feel it is a land in which we could happily settle.

There is a good deal of nervousness at this time about the likelihood of war. Hitler is re-arming Germany and Mussolini is marching about making noises. When he invades Abyssinia there is instant panic, total blackout, lots of marching, shouting and occasional letting off of guns. We have no idea what is happening, nor has anyone the time to explain. It turns out to be not a war but a false alarm. We leave Belgrade with regret and set forth on the long train ride to Bucharest.

CHAPTER XII

LOCKED UP IN RUMANIA!

Bucharest is not that easily reached, as an early hazard arises. We arrive at the Rumanian frontier in the evening. As is usual, an official comes along the train and collects everyone's passports, after which there is a very long wait. We are just thinking of making some tea, when two policemen arrive, shouting to us,

"Off train! Off train!" and bundle us and our belongings onto the platform before marching us to a small cell like room with an iron door, which they shut with a clang. We look around and see that the only furniture in this hole is one hard chair. It is no place to spend what might very well turn out to be the night, so we begin to bang on the door and shout.

"Let us out! Let us out! We don't want to stay here! Let us out at once!" After a while someone comes to see what is going on.

"What is all this? Why are we locked up? What are we supposed to have done?"

"Visas all wrong. No come in Rumania. Tomorrow go back to Belgrade."

"We no sleep here. No beds, no chairs, no WC."

He goes off, presumably to consult someone, and comes back with what appears to be the station-master.

"We lock you tonight. Wait Salle." And they do. The 'Wait Salle' is not too bad at all. There are benches, a table and a WC. We cook a simple meal and do a little dance for them when they come to see if we are still alive. Next we go back to Belgrade, a great waste of time and money, to get our visas sorted out by the chargé d'affairs. Next time there is no problem of entry. We never have any trouble with customs as we always pack our publicity pictures in the top of our trunk. The officials are so tickled with these and so busy calling all their friends to come and have a look, that they never think of looking through our things.

Bucharest is a lovely city, all cream and pink stucco. It is like living in the middle of a wedding cake, a very, very hot one. There are peasants in national dress everywhere, looking very un-westernised, lots of them having stalls in the big market, where they sell not only vegetables, but embroideries of many kinds and all sorts of craft work. We do our household shopping here, armed with pencil and paper to draw what we want if we can't see it. It is very difficult to draw jam. I have got really friendly with a family whose stall is on my daily route and who try to tempt me with embroidered bits and pieces at ever-lower bargain prices, shrieking with laughter at my attempts to communicate.

Elaine wears the Hungarian embroidered dress.

We have a lovely big room with a long balcony along which comes a nice little dog, who likes to play with us. It is in a very big flat with several rooms giving onto a central hall. Lots of girls are about, very often in wrappers. We also seem to meet a lot of men in the lift. After a bit the penny drops. This is a brothel, but no matter, it doesn't bother us.

The cabaret is in a converted country house in a big garden in which we try to cool off between shows, as the heat is terrific, and makes dancing very exhausting. This is a rather up-market joint so we do not make any friends among the clients. June has a seemingly rich and (fairly) handsome boy friend who takes her out a lot, leaving me to explore the interesting old town. He really turns up trumps when he gets off work for a week and takes us up to Sinaia in the mountains and pays for us both to stay in a small hotel. He and June go off all day but I go for walks in the pine forest in the heavenly cool.

It is at this point, as I am wondering what Sofia will be like, that disaster strikes. June gets terribly homesick. She cries and cries and says she simply can't, just can't go any further. This is terribly disappointing but there is nothing to be done but ring up the agent, explain the situation and see if he can fix up anything for us to do on our way home. He is very understanding and helpful. We are fixed for two weeks at a cinema in Zagreb.

What a journey lies ahead, but June's boy friend comes up trumps again. We want to fly as far as Belgrade but can't afford all the fare. He pays part of it and for our excess baggage. This is quite an adventure as it is early days for passenger flights in this part of the world, neither of us has ever flown and this trip is reputed to be extremely dangerous. However, all goes well. It is all a very dramatic flight, quite low over the mountains and giving us great views of the famous Iron Gates, where the Danube squeezes through a narrow gorge in the mountains.

Zagreb seems duller than ever. I think sadly of Sofia and the bookings I had hoped to make on to Athens, maybe the Lebanon and home through the Med. The only thing of note in that fortnight is the amazing reception we get after every performance. I don't think the people had ever seen live entertainment before and they clap and cheer so we can hardly get off stage. Before leaving we go to the market where we buy some beautiful, embroidered local costumes as a finale to our tour.

Sinaia mountains.

EPILOGUE

Back home, after a short break we met in London to do a tour of the agents, which was very disappointing. There seemed to be no call for small acts any more and even cabaret was not offered. The only thing would be to go back to the Continent, which June would not do. In any case, we have done this act long enough and need to think of something else.

I stayed with my family in Cambridge and got a library job for some months before going on a Hellenic cruise to Greece with my parents where I met my future husband. Marriage, children and then the war put a stop to my dancing career.

June stayed in Manchester for a while, then joined two girls, identical twins, who did a novelty act. She incorporated some of our material into their show, which did reasonably well on the variety circuit. June got tired of them and left when asked by Roy Allen to join *The Allen Brothers* whose "June" was leaving. This act was comedy adagio in which June was thrown about in a most terrifying manner, the "brother" being the pianist who was dragged into the act and couldn't (apparently) manage. This ran until the war, when the Allen brothers were called up and June went into an ENSA revue and had a horrible time going to places where no dancer had been before. After the war *The Allen Brothers & June* re-formed and were very successful getting as far as the London Palladium;

Over the years June and I always kept in touch, meeting wherever possible, until her death from cancer in 1972. We were like sisters and I shall always miss her.

June and Elaine.

APPENDIX ONE

THE THEATRES

Theatres and other venues in which Elaine and June danced.

Fraser & Chaytor, alias *Two Regular Guys,* appeared in theatres, cinemas, cabarets and clubs between 1933 and 1937. Elaine kept a detailed diary of engagements for 1934/5 and in her memoirs, lists theatres she remembers dancing in. (m) There are some details on theatre posters and programmes (p) (few of which give the year!) and on agents' contracts ©, but for other years the dates are more vague.

Though a number of these theatres do survive, often metamorphosed into something very far from the old days of the music hall, many have sadly been demolished taking part of our theatrical history with them. The memories of the acts that trod their boards are a vivid reminder of the days of real live entertainment.

Aberdeen – Beach Pavilion (August 1934) (m)
The wooden pavilion was built in 1882 and rebuilt in brick and stone in 1928, as a multi purpose venue for tea dances and summer concert parties, when it became famous for variety. It is now a restaurant.

Alfreton – The Royal (June 1934) ©
The Royal Theatre was a cinema owned by Picture Houses (Derby) Ltd opened in 1931, seating 1750. Changed to The Odeon in 1936 but closed in 1964 and demolished to make way for a supermarket.

Barnet – The Thatched Barn (m)
A restaurant offering regular cabaret shows. Still operated as a restaurant in the 1960s, though without the cabaret.

Barrow – Royalty Theatre and Opera House (June 1933) (p)
Originally the Royal Alhambra Palace and Music Hall (Arthur Worrall), opened on New Years day, 1872, "gaseliers and candelabra superb . . . . upholstery exquisite . . . . architectural arrangements and acoustics perfect" (The Daily Times 2.1.1872). The first home of musical comedy in the 19th century the theatre was reconstructed and refurbished in 1894, opening as the Royalty Theatre and Opera House. The 1920s saw the finest days of repertory here and many famous names trod the stage. The Royalty closed in 1937.

Bradford – The Kings (m)
Elaine remembered appearing at "The Kings" but there does not appear to have been a Kings in Bradford at that time. Could the venue where they danced have been the Kings' Hall and Winter Gardens, Ilkley? Mainly used for theatrical productions, the buildings have been host to variety shows and are still in use today.

Bruton – The Empress (October 1934) (m)

Birkenhead – The Argyll (September 1934) (m)
The Argyll was built in 1868. Destroyed by a bomb and closed in 1940.

Blackpool – The Alhambra (m)
Built in 1899 by Wylson and Long. Demolished in 1961.

Bolton – The Hippodrome (m)
Built in 1908 and demolished in 1961.

Bootle – Metropole (March 1934) (m)
Designed in 1910 in the Renaissance style (Havelock, Sutton & Sons), it had an impressive and ornate, five story façade 80ft wide, with an iron and glass verandah. Seating 1,850, the design allowed a fine view from every seat. The artistic décor featured white plaster-work, offset by crimson walls and seats. Extensive alterations and improvements took place in 1922 and in 1931 and in 1934 cinema, reviews and variety shows were put on. The theatre was destroyed by a German bomb on May 7th 1941.

Buxton – The Royal (June 1934) (m)
Built in 1871 and later demolished.

Cambridge – ADC Theatre (1933) (p)
Opened in 1860 in a set of rooms by the Amateur Dramatic Club – the oldest amateur run theatre in the 20th century. Larger rooms were purchased and a gallery built in 1866. Structural improvement in 1888. In 1933 part of the theatre was burnt down (this must have been after Elaine's appearance there) and was rebuilt in 1935. The ADC still operates as a theatre, mainly for student productions.

Castleford – New Theatre of Varieties (May 1933) (p)
Listed in the Castleford Official Guide c1932 as the "only theatre in Castleford". There were two theatres, the Queen's and the Royal, in Castleford as well as a number of "picture palaces" but about 1932, when talking pictures came to the town, the Castleford Royal took over presenting variety shows. This is probably why the 1933 poster advertises the "New Theatre of Varieties". Built in the last quarter of the 19th century, the Royal had a long history of presenting high-class drama, opera and variety until it closed in 1953. It was demolished in the 1960s to make way for a supermarket.

Chester – The Royalty (m)
Built in 1882 (B.E. Entwistle) on the site of a wooden building used for circuses. The exterior is of plain, painted brick. About 960 people were accommodated in the auditorium in stalls, circle, gallery supported by pillars with round-fronted boxes at circle level each side of the proscenium. The theatre later became a cinema and in 1958 the stage was altered for pop concerts. In 1960 it was converted for bingo, closing in 1966. The foyer and hospitality parts of the theatre are now a nightclub while the auditorium is disused.

Crewe – The New Theatre (m)
Now known as The Lyceum, this theatre has had many name changes. In 1882 a disused catholic church was converted into the first Lyceum Theatre. Alfred Darbyshire designed a new theatre, seating 1250, built on the church site, which opened in 1889. This was destroyed by fire in 1910 and was completely re-built as the New Theatre. The building was extended and improved in 1994 and continues as a working theatre with further up-grades planned. The red brick façade is not much altered while the pleasing decoration of the auditorium has been carefully retained in the refurbishment.

Dover – The Royal Hippodrome (m)
Designed by Phipps in 1897. Demolished in 1957.

Eccles – Broadway (April 1934) (p)

Fleetwood – The Palace (April 1934) (m)
Built in 1908 and closed in 1937. Demolished in the 1970s.

Hastings – The Pavilion (m)
Also known as the Pier Pavilion it was built in 1881 and closed in 1939. Demolished in 1951.

Hull – The Tivoli (April 1934) (p)
Little is known about this theatre, designed by Smith, and demolished in 1959.

Lancaster – The Palace (m)
This must be a different theatre to the Palace of Varieties, which was destroyed by fire in 1907, some years before Elaine visited it!

Lincoln – The Theatre Royal (May 1933) (p)
The New Theatre was built in 1806 over a former burial ground. This was replaced in 1893 by the present building designed by Bertie Crew. The entrance and frontage was rebuilt in 1945 but the original plasterwork still gives character to the auditorium, which continues to host touring theatre companies.

Liverpool – The Pavilion (July 1934) (m)
Built in 1908 (Alley) and refurbished in 1933. The stage was extended in 1960 and in 1961 the theatre was converted for bingo. Most of the building was destroyed by fire in 1986.

London, Brixton – The Empress (Brixton Theatre) (October 1934) (m)
Built in 1898 (Wylson & Long). Radical reconstruction in 1931, converted to a cinema (David Nye) in 1956 and demolished 1993.

London – Burlington Gardens Club (p)

London, East Ham – The Palace (m)
Built in 1906 (Wylson & Long). Closed in 1940s and demolished in 1958.

London, Hammersmith – The Palace (m)
> Opened in 1932 (Robert Cromie) as a cinema seating 3579. The very wide frontage is accessed by nine pairs of double doors. The auditorium and proscenium are correspondingly wide and capacious. The fine art-deco design, incorporating repeated aediculed motifs, is retained. The organ chamber was, unusually, above the stage but the organ is now in store. In 1999 the theatre became The Apollo and is now used as a theatre and concert hall.

London, Old Kent Road – The Globe (January 1934) (m)

London, Poplar – Queen's Theatre (April 1934) ©
> Opened in 1856 as the "Queen's Arms Palace of Varieties and Public House" seating 800. Altered to become the 'Apollo' music hall in 1873. Reconstructed in 1898 (Bertie Crewe) with a capacity of 1360 as the 'Albion Theatre'. In 1922 became The 'Oriental Theatre' which changed to the 'Queen's Music Hall', and was altered again in 1937 to become the 'Queen's Theatre of Varieties'. Closed in 1958 and demolished in 1964.

London, Regent Street – The Monico (February 1934) (m)

London, Regent Street – Mitre Club (April 1934) (m)

London, Walthamstow – The Palace (November 1934) (m)
> Built in 1903 by Wylson and Long. Closed in 1954 and demolished 1960.

London, West Ham – Hippodrome (m)

London, Woolwich – The Empire (p)
> Opened 1935 as the West Kent Theatre replacing the 1834 'The New Portable Theatre'. 1837 became 'Duchess of Kent's Theatre', 1892 'Barnard's Theatre' under management of Samuel Barnard. Reconstructed by Frank Matcham in 1899 with a capacity of 1450. 1932 called 'The Woolwich Empire'. Closed and demolished 1960.

Manchester – Pend. ? (March 1934) (m)

Manchester – The Dominion (February 1934) (m)

Middlesburgh – The Empire (p)
> Built in 1899 (Ernest Runtz), in 'Spanish Renaissance' style with terracotta frontage and a series of arched windows. Originally had two towers but these were not replaced after bomb damage in the Second World War. The fine and intimate auditorium seated 1100 and features rich and delicate renaissance detail. The theatre is now a themed pub.

Prestatyn – The Alhambra (m)
> The Alhambra Restaurant was not in Prestatyn but in nearby Rhyl. On the Ocean Beach site facing the promenade, it had seating for 1000 and a stage on which many cabaret and variety acts played in the 1920s and 30s. The Alhambra later became the Ritz Ballroom, destroyed by fire in 1968.

Redcar – The Pavilion (m)
> The New Pavilion Theatre in Redcar still stands and is now the Regent Cinema.

Rochdale – The Carlton (November 1934) (m)

The Carlton, a superior Ballroom, Café and Restaurant, opened on September 19th 1934 – quite new when Elaine and June danced in the cabaret there. The spring floor of Canadian maple took over 400 couples, while for those not dancing, the balcony seated another 300 people. There was a resident band and the Cabaret changed weekly. The Carlton is now the venue for Liquid Rock – rather different from the music of the thirties!

Shotton – Alhambra (June 1934) (c)

St Helens – Hippodrome (February 1934) (m)

Stockport – Theatre Royal (May 1934) (c)

Built in 1888 (Matcham), closed in 1957. Demolished 1960.

Tynemouth – Palace by the Sea – Ballroom (July 1934) (m)

Built 1878 (Norton and Massey) Closed in 1960s and demolished 1998.

Uxbridge – Regal Cinema (November 1933) (c)

Opened 1931 (E. Norman Bailey) in an exotic, flamboyant Art Deco style. Behind "Egyptian" style frontage is a spacious and elegantly decorated interior. The auditorium, in "stadium" style seated 1,700 and features elaborate decoration enhanced by concealed lighting. There was also a ballroom and café. An excellent Compton organ was installed in the pit. Presented a full programme of films, variety acts, children's entertainment and concerts but audiences dwindled, forcing closure in 1977. Auditorium now used as a nightclub, ballroom a snooker hall and backstage area a fitness club. As a listed building, Bailey's interior décor has been preserved.

Warrington – The Queens Cinema (m)

Owned by Orford Lane (Warrington) Picture House Ltd typical of the period before 1914. A lavish design with impressive façade and fine glass and iron canopy. 33ft wide proscenium with auditorium seating 1,179 people. In 1930 with Western Electric sound it became The Queen's Talkie Picture Theatre. Variety shows were put on between the films. Closed in 1960 and in 1962 demolished to make way for a petrol station.

York – Theatre Royal (p)

Built in 1756 (architect unknown). Underwent no less than six reconstructions, the last in 1994 (Allen Tod). Still functions as a producing and touring theatre. Much of the Georgian building still survives though the present stone façade dates from 1880 (George Styan) in a Victorian gothic style. The auditorium and stage date from 1902 and are spacious yet intimate. Much of the decoration is in imaginative Art Nouveau style.

Ireland, Belfast – The Empire (May 1934) (c)

Opened in 1894 as The Empire Theatre of Varieties, which replaced a much smaller, earlier theatre. Built by the impresario, Dan Lowry, it soon became known for high-class entertainment. In 1896 the first living pictures to be seen in Belfast, "The Marvellous, Perplexing and Original Luminere Cinematographe", caused much excitement. The Empire flourished well into the 20th century combining Music Hall, Variety, Cinema and Plays (being home to the Empire Players and the Belfast Rep Co.), attracting many well known performers. In spite of very successful performances of plays in 1960 the Empire closed in 1961 and was demolished in 1962.

Ireland, Cork – The Opera House (May 1934) (c)

Opened 1855 (architect Sir John Benson) as a centre for meetings, museum, concerts and theatre but not a success due to poor acoustics. Re-modelled 1873 and named "Munster Hall". 1877 re-designed by C. J. Phipps for "The Great & Royal Opera Co." which wound up in 1888 when Cork Opera House established. The turn of the 20th century saw the days of grand opera with many well-known companies visiting. The Opera House was destroyed by fire in 1955, rebuilt in 1963 and renovated and refurbished in 1993. It remains a centre of cultural and social life of Cork City.

Ireland, Dublin – The Olympia (May 1934) (c)

In 1879 Dan Lowry opened the Star of Erin Music Hall on the site of the old Crampton Court Theatre. It later became the Empire Palace and in the 20th century, the Olympia. In the 1890s a new entrance was added, with the wonderful cast iron and stained glass canopy, which can still be enjoyed today. The theatre is known for the elaborately decorated interior. It is the finest Victorian theatre remaining in Dublin and is host to concerts, plays and pantomimes.

Antwerp – The Globe (October 1934) (m)

Belgrade – Palace (September 1935) (m)

Brussels – El Mexicano (May 1935) (m)

Brussels – The Gaiety (September 1934) (m)

Brussels – The Hungarica (March 1935) (m)

Brussels – The Kasak (April 1935) (m)

Brussels – The Parisienne (February 1935) (m)

Bucharest – Maxims (August 1935) (m)

Budapest – Moulin Rouge (July 1935) (m)

Budapest – Roseland (m)

Knocke – Phare (June 1935) (m)

Luxembourg – Pole Nord Hotel (November/December 1934) (m)

BIBLIOGRAPHY

Ackroyd, Harold. – The Liverpool Stage
BBC – The Empire Theatre Belfast
     BBC 'Famous Music Halls' 1938
Byrne, Ophelia – The Stage in Ulster from the Eighteenth Century.
     The Linen Hall Library
Earl, John & Sell, Michael – Guide to British Theatres 1750–1950
     The Theatres Trust
Gibbon, William M. – A Change of Scene.
Howard, Diana- London Theatres and Music Halls. 1850–1950
     The Library Association.
Jones, Colin - Rhyl Holiday History c. 1800–2000
Mellor, Geoff. J. - Bradford & District Theatres and Music Halls
Morash, Christopher - History of Irish Theatre 1601–2000
     Cambridge University Press 2002
Pearson, Peter – Heart of Dublin. Resurgance of an Historic City
     O'Brian Press 2000
Rochdale County Borough Directory 1934
Roddis, David – The Thrill of it All:
     the story of cinema in Ilkeston and the Eerewash Valley.
Hornsey Brian – Ninety Years of Cinema in Warrington.
     1998
Skinner, James – Hillingdon Cinemas (Images of England Series)
     Tempest Publications 2002

Many thanks to everyone who has helped furnish details of the venues. So much fascinating information about these amazing buildings and their history, including original advertisements and reviews, could make a lengthy book. Sadly, it has only been possible to include a few notes on each here. Special thanks to staff of the Local Studies Departments of numerous public libraries who took so much trouble to research and send material. Their interest and time has been much appreciated.

Le Bar Kasak – Bruxelles.

THE ARTISTS

Elaine and June generally appeared as "FRASER AND CHAYTOR" (though theatre posters and playbills were very free with their names – June was often Joan; Chaytor was spelt Chayter, Chater, and even Taylor! One wonders if theatres could get away with this in these days of litigation?)
They were subtitled variously:

Two Regular Guys

Two Guys

Two Regular Guys in a Dancing Potpourri

The Personality Girls – *With a Novel and Dainty Offering*

Some Steppers!

Potty enough to do anything!

Two Charming Girls who Dance

Comedy Duo

Personality and Rhythm Girls

ARTISTS AND ACTS

Who shared the stage with Elaine and June.

ALEC DAIMLER & DORA EADIE – *Going all out* – *Tearing after him!*

ALMA MACKAY – *Famous Speciality Dancer*

ALPLEON – *Yells and Yodels!*

ANGELE MAGUIRE – *Violin*

ARCHIES JUVENILE BAND – *The Youngest Band in the World*

ARNOLD & ARCHIE – *Crazy Equilibrists*

BABY LOVE – *The Living Doll.*

BALVERA TRIO – *Thrills on Wheels* – *Dare-devil Skating by Basil & Vera.*

BEREL & OSTRAN – *Versatile Comedy Couple* – *Singing, Dancing & Patter*

BERT LLOYD and Partner

BERT LOMAN – *Jovial Compere*

CAMILLE GILLARD – *The Famous Belgian Tenor*

CHARLIE MANNY & VIC ROBERTS – *The Messenger Boys*

CHUNGLING SEN – *The Mandarin of Mystery. A Whirlwind of Deception*

CLARA MONAGHAN – *The Lancashire Singing Mill Girl*

EDDIE BOWERS – *The BBC Recording Star*

ETHEL COLYER GIRLS – *A Sextet of pretty Girls with Gorgeous Costumes*

EVELYN HARDY and her LADIES BAND – *England's greatest Lady Trumpeter*

FIVE MELODISTEN – (Luxembourg 1934)

FOUR ACES

FOUR COLONIALS featuring PRINCESS IWA – *in Songs, Dance & Comedy*

FRANK KEITH – *his latest success*

FRED BREZIN – *Magician and Pickpocket*

G.H. CARLISLE – *Versatile Entertainer*

HAROLD BOWMER – *Singer*

HARVEY SELINE TRIO – *The Famous Trio*

HASSAN – *The Merry Wizard*

HAVER & LEE – *The Fun Racketeers*

HELEN BINNIE – *Comedy Cameo*

HUBERT VALENTINE – *Ireland's Leading Tenor*

JACK MARTELL – *Vaudeville's Cocktail*

JACK STOCKS – *The Woman Hater*

JEAN KENNEDY – *Scotland's Comedy Star*

JOAN D'ARCY – *The Golden Voiced Soprano*

JOE ADAMI – *The Human Billiard Table* – *Expert Conjuror*

JOE KAY'S BURLINGTON BAND

JOHNNY GAY – *Burlesque Comedian*

JOHNNY WATSON'S Pretty Smart Canine Wonders & Clever Performing Donkey – *Through "Dogged" Determination have been a "Howling" Success Everywhere.*

KNIGHT and DAY – *The Two Laughter Makers. Entertainers at the Piano*

LAURIE & RAYNE – *Sticky fingers! No Foolin'*

LES 4 PAULETTES – *The Sensation of the Age*

LES BEAUCAIRES – *Comedy Juggling Entertainers*

LIELA DEE – *Krazy to Sing* – *and does!*

LIEUTENANT ZAALOFF'S CAUCASION ENTERTAINERS

LILLIAN CLAY – *The Canadian Comedienne*

LIONEL'S CLUB ORCHESTRA – (Liege & Ostende 1935)

LOWE and LOWMAN – *Comedians by Nature*

MAUDIE EDWARDS – *Comedienne - Songs and Impressions*

MINIATURE MILITARY MUSICIANS

P.S. BRYANT – *piano accompanist*

RIO & SANTOS – *Two Argentine Gentlemen of Riotous Habits*

SAMSON – *The Original and Amazing! The Strongest man in the World whose Marvellous feats of Strength have Thrilled the Whole Universe. Astonishing! Miraculous!*

SERENO & JUNE – *Equilibrists par excellence*

SKEETS MARTIN – *The Well Known Character Comedian*

STEPHAN – *The Armless Wonder*

SYBIL SCANES – *Lyric Soprano*

SYLVESTER and his NEPHEWS – *Neatest of the Neat in Sidewalks of New York*

TEDDY STREAM – *Characterising Comedian*

THE 2 VAN DE PEEARS with MISS SUSIE – *the Act Unique*

THE GLADIATORS

THREE ZAROVS – *Extraordinary Balancing Feats*

THE TOBY FAMILY – *The Cleverest Monkeys and Dogs in the World*

TWENTY MASTERSINGERS – *A Musical Sensation. A Masterpiece of Melody.*

TWO SHARPES – *Sailors who play on Any Quay*

VAN DUSEN – *England's Premier Character Y*

WALKER & BRACEGIRDLE – *With Vocal Gems & Absurdities*

YVONNE – *Wonderful girl acrobat. Refined Comedy. Acrobatic Speciality.*

The Five Melodisten.

LIST OF ILLUSTRATIONS